AF598977

# Greetings and Phrases

by E. Russell Primm III • illustrated by Kathleen Petelinsek

childsworld.com

**Published by The Child's World®**
800-599-READ • childsworld.com



**Photography Credits**
PeopleImages.com–Yuri A/Shutterstock.com, cover; Monkey Business Images/Shutterstock.com, 1, 9, 17; supparsorn/Shutterstock.com, 3; Roman Samborskyi/Shutterstock.com, 4; ANURAK PONGPATIMET/Shutterstock.com, 5; Krakenimages.com/Shutterstock.com, 6, 12; Asier Romero/Shutterstock.com, 7; Pavel L Photo and Video/Shutterstock.com, 8; Pixel-Shot/Shutterstock.com, 10; fizkes/Shutterstock.com, 11, 18, 19; Yuliya Evstratenko/Shutterstock.com, 13; Prostock-studio/Shutterstock.com, 14; Riccardo Mayer/Shutterstock.com, 15; Amir Bajric/Shutterstock.com, 16; Gyorgy Barna/Shutterstock.com, 20; engagestock/Shutterstock.com, 21

**ISBN Information**
9781503889033 (Reinforced Library Binding)
9781503890114 (Portable Document Format)
9781503891357 (Online Multi-user eBook)
9781503892590 (Electronic Publication)

**LCCN** 2023950372

**Printed in the United States of America**

**Note to Parents, Caregivers, and Educators:** The understanding of any language begins with the acquisition of vocabulary, whether the language is spoken or manual. The books in this series provide readers, both young and old, with basic American Sign Language signs. Combining close photo cues and simple, but detailed, line illustrations, children and adults alike can begin the process of learning American Sign Language.

Let these books be an introduction to the world of American Sign Language. Most languages have regional dialects and multiple ways of expressing the same thought. This is also true for sign language. We have attempted to use the most common version of the signs for the words in this series. As with any language, the best way to learn is to be taught in person by a frequent user. It is our hope that this series will pique your interest in sign language.

**A special thanks to our advisers:** As a member of a deaf family that spans four generations, **Kim Bianco Majeri** lives, works, and plays among the Deaf community. **Carmine L. Vozzolo** is an educator of children who are deaf and hard of hearing, as well as their families.

**E. Russell Primm III** was a well-known figure in the publishing industry who produced thousands of acclaimed books for children. He was affiliated with organizations such as the American Library Association, the Chicago Book Clinic, and the University of Chicago Publishing Program Advisory Board.

**Kathleen Petelinsek** has loved books since she was a child. Through the years, she has written, designed, and illustrated many books for children. She lives in Wisconsin, near her granddaughter who also shares her love for books.

If you wear a watch, just pointing to it will make this sign.

# What time is it?

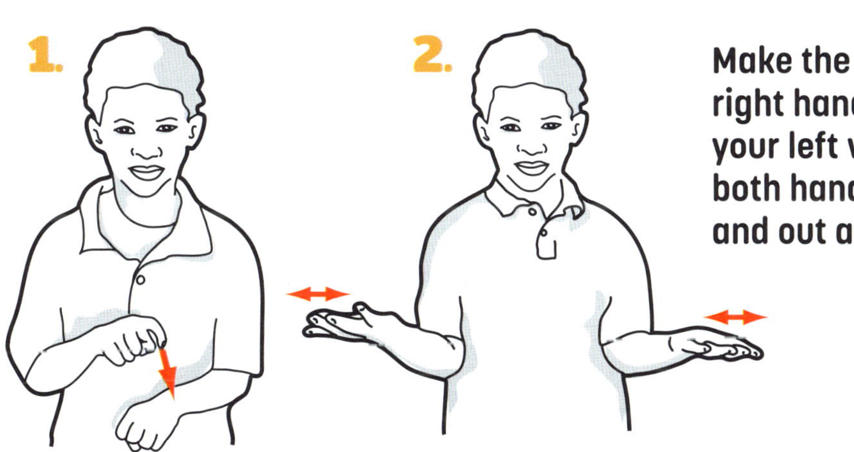


Make the "X" sign with your right hand. Tap the back of your left wrist twice. Then open both hands and move them in and out at the same time.

"Hello" in Spanish is "Hola" (OH-la).

# Hello.

This sign is like a small salute. Place your hand on your forehead close to your ear, and move it outward and away from your body. Be sure to smile!

"Goodbye" in French is "Au revoir" (OH ruh-VWAR).

# Goodbye.

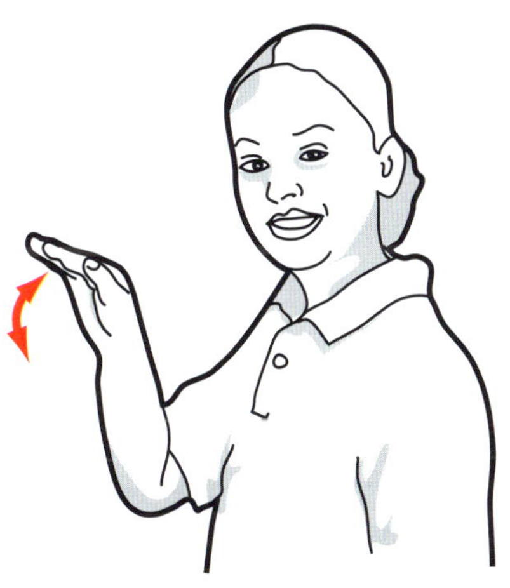

Open your palm, fold down your fingers, and then open your palm again.

Names sometimes have meanings. The meaning can change with different languages.

# What is your name?

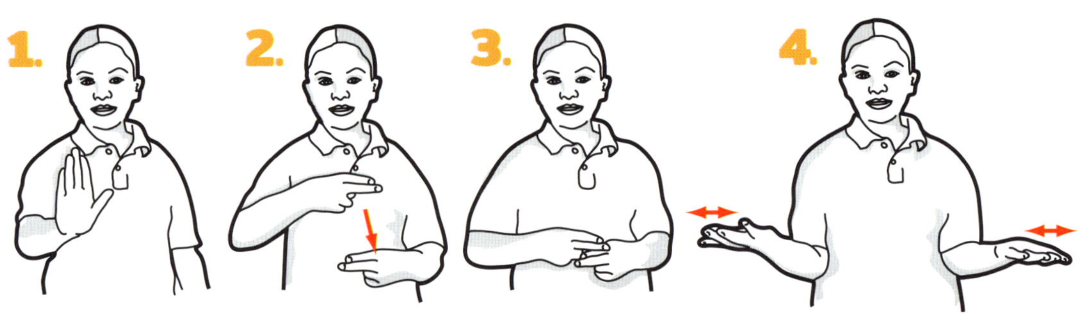


Face your flat right hand out. Then make the "H" shape with both hands and tap your fingers together. Face your hands up and move them in and out at the same time.

Can you sign your name? Check out the chart on page 23!

# My name is . . .

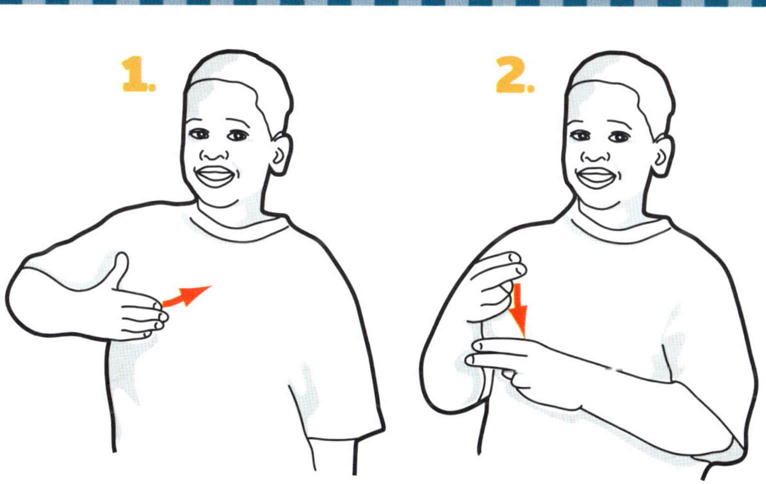


Pat your chest with your flat right hand. Then make the "H" shape with both hands and tap them together.

Asking "How are you?" is a nice way to greet someone.

# How are you?

Bend your fingers (both hands) toward your chest. Then rotate your hands so your fingers point up. Now point your right index finger at the person you're talking to.

1\.

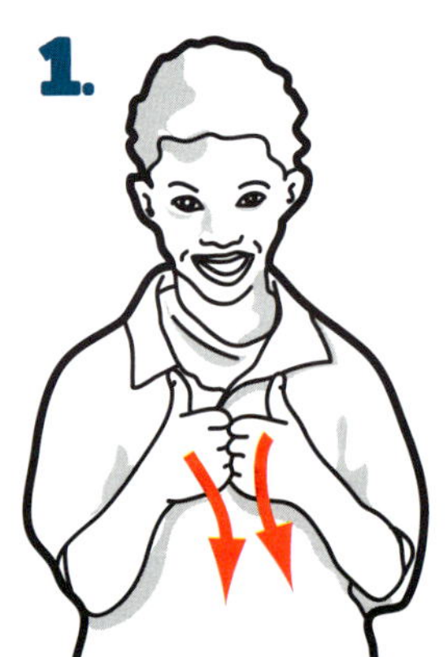

2\.

3\.

Saying "I'm OK" is another way to say "I'm fine."

# I'm fine.

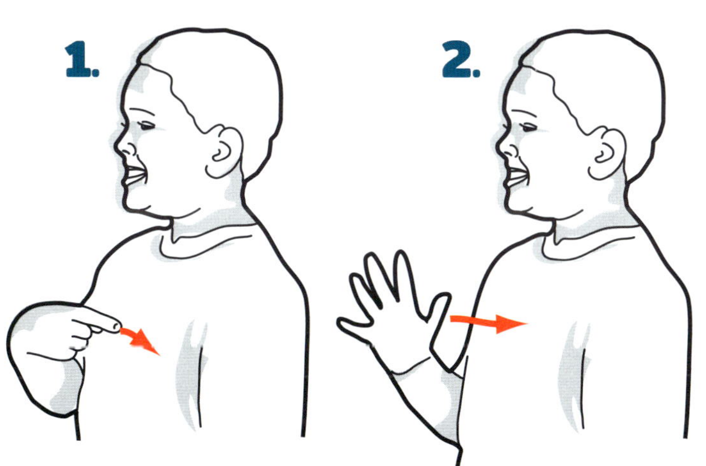


Tap your chest with your right index finger. Then open your right hand and tap your chest twice with your right thumb.

"Thank you" in Japanese is "Arigato" (ah-ree-GAH-toh).

# Thank you.

Put your flat right hand on your chin. Then move it down and away.

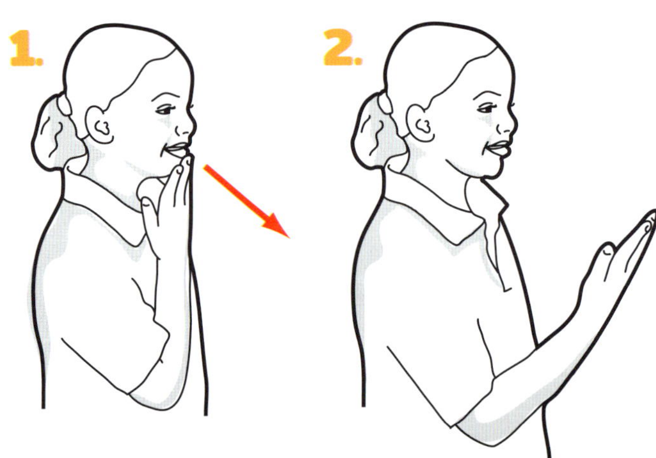

"You're welcome" in Spanish is "De nada" (DAY NAH-dah).

# You're welcome.

1.

2.

Flatten your right hand and move it toward your stomach.

"Please" in German is "Bitte" (BIH-teh).

# Please.

Put your flat right hand on your chest. Move it in a circular motion.

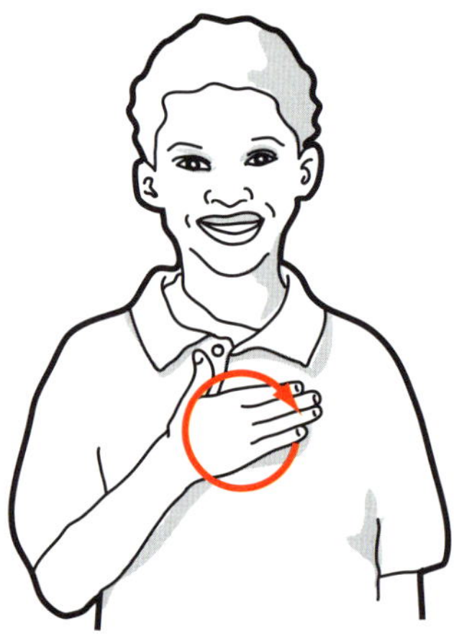

"Excuse me" in French is "Excusez-moi" (ek-SKOOZ-ay MWAH).

# Excuse me.

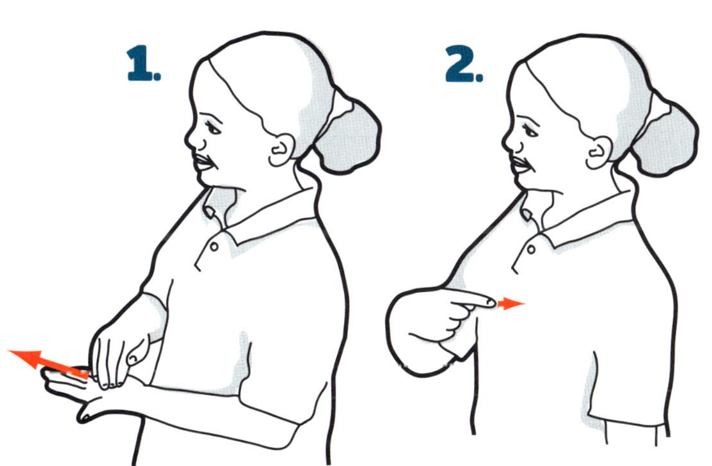


Bend the fingers on your right hand. Slide them off your flattened left hand. Then tap your right index finger on your chest.

"Yes" in German is "Ja" (YAH).

# Yes.

Make the "S" sign with your right hand. Move your wrist downward a few times while nodding your head "yes."

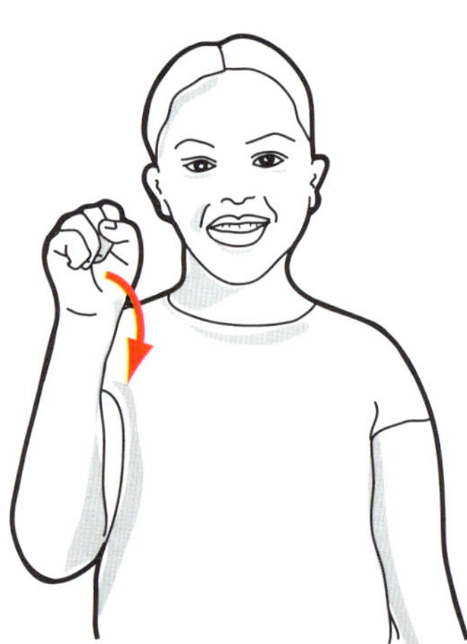

"No" means the same thing in many languages!

# No.

Touch the middle and index fingers of your right hand to your thumb while shaking your head "no."

A handshake is an easy way to meet someone.

## Nice to meet you.

Start with your flat left hand facing up. Keep it still while your flat right hand slides across and off. Then make the "1" sign with both hands. Touch your hands together. Then point at the person you're meeting.

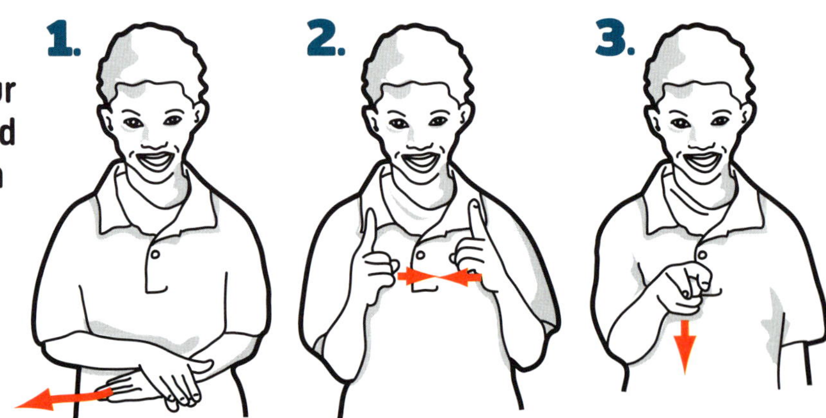

Practice this sign with a friend!

# I like you.

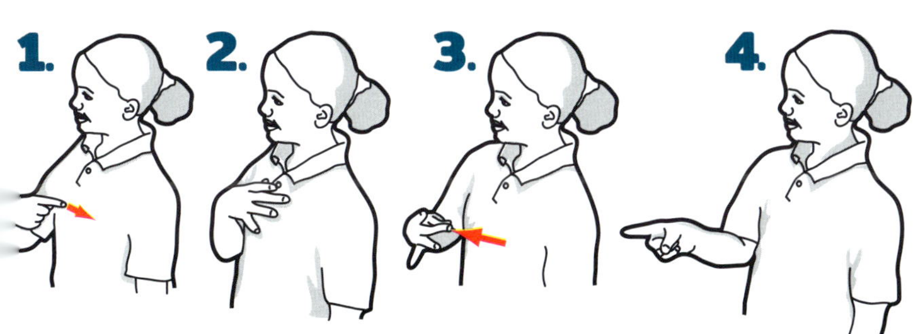


Tap your chest with your right index finger. Then touch your thumb and middle finger to your chest. Pull away and close your thumb and middle finger together. Now point to the person you are talking to.

"Help me" in French is "Aidez-moi" (ED-ay MWAH).

# Help!

Make a fist with your right hand, keeping your thumb up. Put your flat left hand underneath and push up.

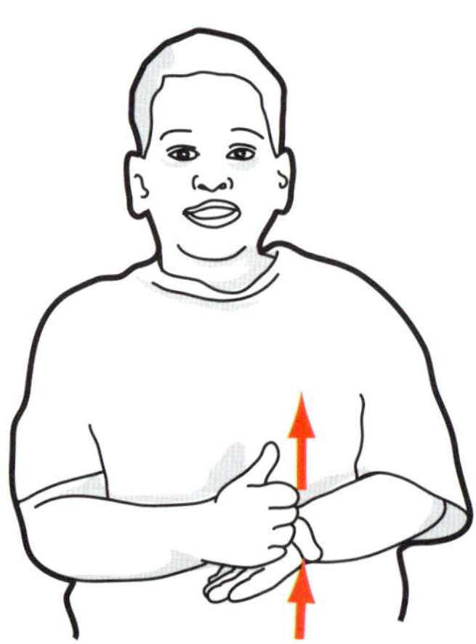

"I'm sorry" in Spanish is "Lo siento" (LOH see-EN-toh).

# I'm sorry.

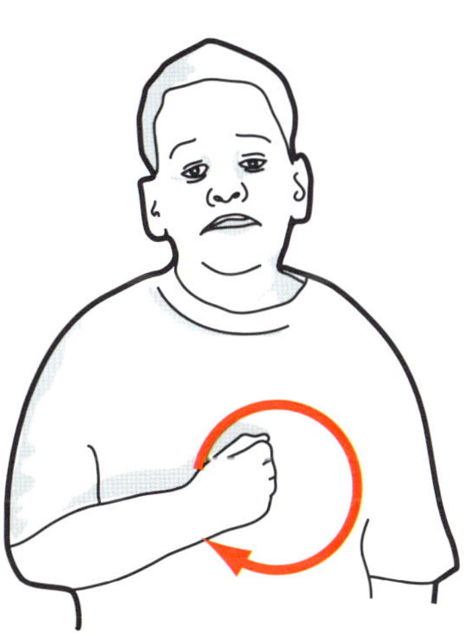

Make the "A" sign with your right hand. Then make a circular movement on your chest.

"Good morning" in Japanese is "Ohayoo" (oh-HY-oh).

# Good morning.

Flatten both of your hands and face them toward you. Touch your right hand to your chin, then move it downward into your left hand. Now place your left hand inside your right elbow. Pull your right hand toward your face.

"Good night" in German is "Gute Nacht" (GOO-teh NAKT).

# Good night.

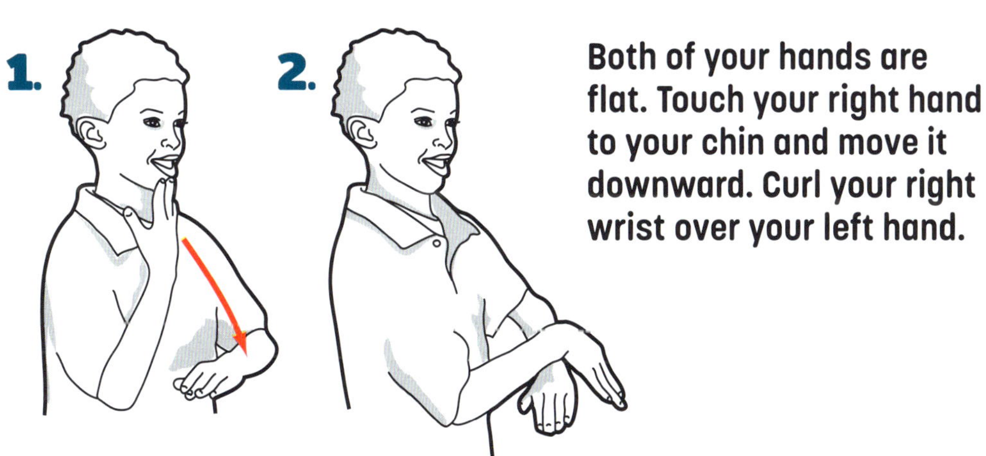


Both of your hands are flat. Touch your right hand to your chin and move it downward. Curl your right wrist over your left hand.

## Wonder More

- How much did you know about American Sign Language (ASL) before reading this book? Do you already know some ASL signs? What new signs did you learn?

- Some words or specific names don't have signs. In these cases, you can spell the individual letters of the word, which is called fingerspelling. Look at the alphabet chart on page 23. Can you sign the letters in your name?

- With a partner, pick three signs from this book and practice them together. Are you able to understand each other? Is ASL easier or harder than you thought it would be?

- Do you think it is important to learn ASL? Why or why not? Where can you learn more signs?

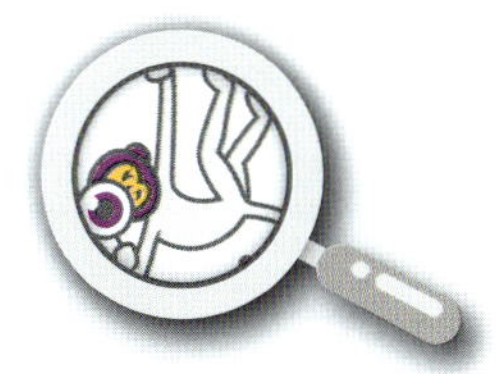

# Sign Language Alphabet

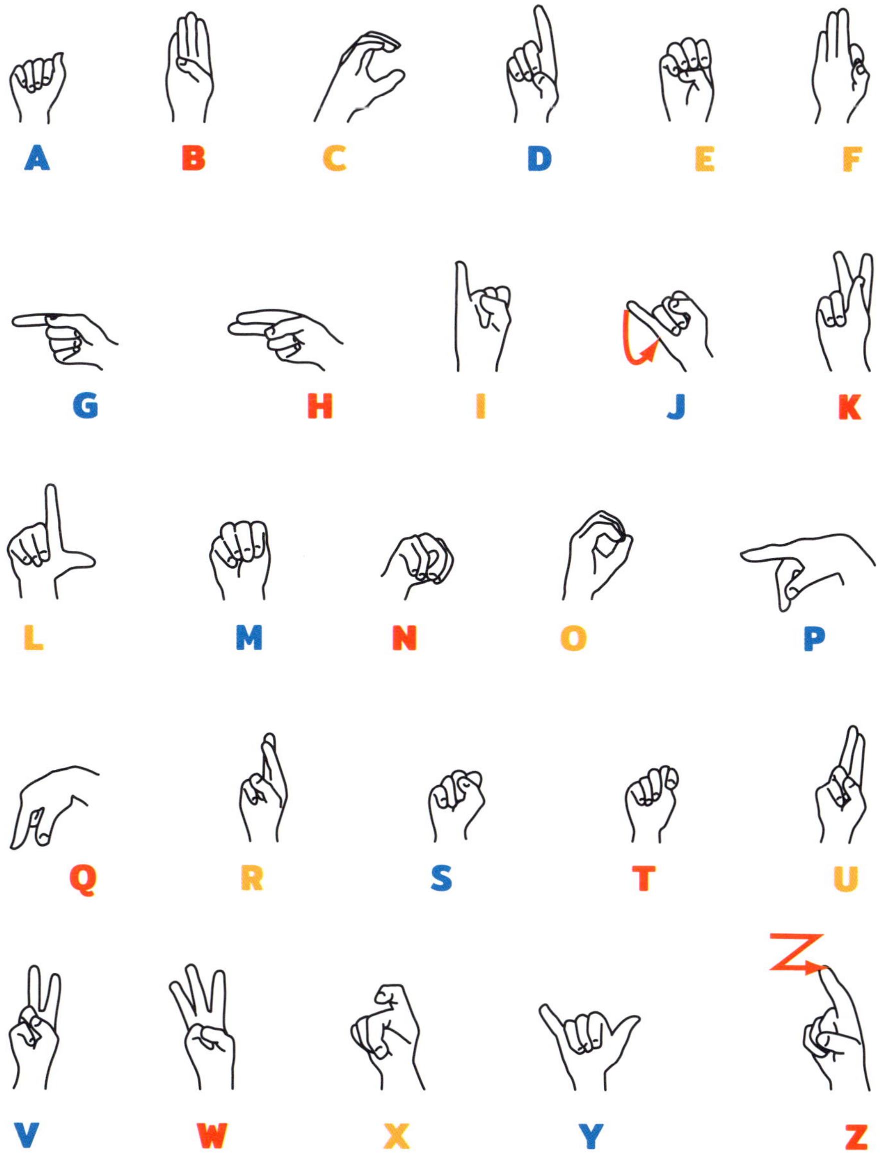

A B C D E F

G H I J K

L M N O P

Q R S T U

V W X Y Z

# Find Out More

## In the Library

Barlow, Rochelle, and Natalia Sanabria (illustrator). *American Sign Language for Kids: 101 Easy Signs for Nonverbal Communication*. Emeryville, CA: Rockridge Press, 2019.

Brakenhoff, Kelly, and Theresa Murray (illustrator). *Never Mind!* (Duke the Deaf Dog ASL Series). Lincoln, NE: Emerald Prairie Press, 2019.

## On the Web

Visit our website for links about American Sign Language:
**childsworld.com/links**

*Note to Parents, Caregivers, Teachers, and Librarians: We routinely verify our web links to make sure they are safe and active sites. So encourage your readers to check them out!*

# A Special Thank-You!

Thank you to our models from the Program for Children Who are Deaf and Hard of Hearing at the Alexander Graham Bell School in Chicago, Illinois.

Alina's favorite things to do are art, soccer, and swimming. DJ is her brother!

DJ loves playing the harmonica and video games. Alina is his sister!

Dareous likes football. His favorite team is the Detroit Lions. He also likes to play video games.